The Star That Shines In You

I0459450

The Star That Shines In You, is a 28-day Christmas bedtime journey revealing that the same light that once shone over Bethlehem now lives within every child of God. Each gentle story unfolds the wonder of Emmanuel—Heaven's glory come to dwell in human hearts. Through quiet nights, shining stars, and simple acts of faith, families discover that Christ's presence is not a memory but a living flame guiding, comforting, and transforming daily life. This book reminds every reader that they are the light-bearers of His Kingdom, that His peace has made their hearts His home, and that no darkness can ever overcome the brightness of His love now shining within them.

Catalog Number: A990
Category: Revelation / Miracles (Declarations)
Body Part: Eyes

The Star That Shines In You

Published by **Discipleship Training International Press**

Scripture quotations are taken from the Holy Bible, King James Version (KJV), public domain.

Printed in the United States of America.

ISBN: 978-1-970550-11-5

First Edition, 2025

Design and layout by Discipleship Training International Press

Discipleship Training International are Trademarks of Isaac Newton Corns.

For permissions or bulk orders, contact:
DiscipleshipTrainingInternational.com

Table of Contents

Day 1: The Promise of a Star

Long before the shepherds watched their flocks by night, God promised a light that would never fade. He spoke through His prophets of a Star that would rise from Jacob, a King who would rule in love and peace. The promise was not about the sky, but about hearts that would shine with His glory. When you look at the night, remember that God's plan was always to bring His light near. He wanted His children to see Him clearly, not far away, but close—so close that His light could live inside them forever.

The same God who promised the Star has already kept His word. When Christ was born in Bethlehem, Heaven's light filled the earth. Angels sang because the time had come for darkness to lose its power. The promise was no longer waiting—it was living. Every ray of that star pointed to Jesus, the true Light of the world. And when you believe in Him, that same light shines in you. It cannot be hidden, because it was given by God Himself. His promise has already come true inside your heart.

You do not have to search the sky to find His light. It is not a faraway star, but the glow of His love in you. Every time you speak kindness, share hope, or forgive, His light shines brighter. Christ's promise has already entered your life. You are not waiting for Him to appear; He already dwells in you. The light that guided the wise men now guides your heart, teaching you to walk in peace and joy every day.

When you wake each morning, you rise with His light. You carry the promise that angels announced long ago. The same power that broke through the night now lives in you. The Star that once hung over Bethlehem never went out—it moved inside His children. Wherever you go, the promise walks with you, bringing warmth to every cold place and light to every dark corner. You are part of God's great shining story.

If the night ever seems too long, remember that the promise has already come. No darkness can stop His light. It glows even when eyes cannot see it, because it burns in the Spirit that Christ placed within you. You are never without His brightness, never without His hope. The promise of the Star lives in you now and forever, because Emmanuel—God with us—has come, and He will never leave.

So rest tonight, knowing the same light that guided shepherds still watches over you. The promise is alive in your heart, steady and sure. God's Word has been fulfilled. The Star still shines, and its name is Jesus. His light has made its home in you, and it will never fade.

Day 2: The Star Appears

When the night was still and quiet, a new light broke through the sky. It was brighter than any star before it, for Heaven itself was announcing the King. The angels rejoiced, and the world was forever changed. That star was not just a sign in the heavens—it was a message to every heart that God's promise had come. The light that shone over Bethlehem was a mirror of what God planned for all His children, that His presence would dwell within them, shining forever with His peace.

The star did not appear for kings or scholars alone; it was for everyone who looked toward Heaven with hope. It told the earth that love had come near. The light was not meant to stay far away—it came to lead. Just as the shepherds followed the glory in the sky, every believer now follows the light of Christ in their heart. You do not wait for signs in the sky; His Spirit leads you from within, showing that the King has already come to dwell with you.

Every sparkle of that star carried the voice of God saying, "Fear not, for I am with you." The light was the proof that God's promise had arrived. It was His way of saying, "My Word has become flesh." The shepherds saw it and believed, and you, too, can rest in that same truth. The Star that once appeared over Bethlehem now appears in every child who believes. You do not need to search the horizon; His glory rises within your spirit and fills your heart with warmth that will never end.

The light of that Star did not fade when the morning came; it simply moved. It moved from the sky into hearts, into families, into the world that needed saving. When Christ came, He brought Heaven's brightness to dwell among His people. The angels' song never stopped—it echoes now through you. Each time you speak kindness or shine peace, the same Star appears again through your life. You have become the living sky that shows the world that God has come.

The Star appeared once to announce the birth of Jesus, but tonight it shines again as you rest in His love. You are part of the great story of light—no darkness can overcome it, no fear can hide it. His presence in you is the light that never dims. You are not small beneath the heavens; the heavens themselves rejoice because His light lives in you. Just as that first Star guided the wise, your life now guides others to see Him.

Rest now, knowing the Star still shines. You do not look upward to find it—you simply believe, and it glows from within. Christ has appeared, and His light fills your world. The same light that guided shepherds and wise men now lights your path. The Star has appeared, and it shines forever in you.

Day 3: The Journey Begins

When the wise men first saw the star, they knew something holy had begun. They packed their treasures and started their journey, following the light that led them toward a promise. They did not know every detail of where the road would take them, but they trusted the One who placed the star in the sky. Every step was guided by faith, not by sight. And in the same way, your life is a journey of faith. You may not see every turn, but the light of Christ within you shows each step you need to take, one moment at a time.

The wise men did not travel alone. They walked together, following the same light. Their unity was born out of one vision—to find the King. In the same way, your family walks together under God's light. You do not walk in darkness or confusion, because His Word has already gone before you. Christ in you is the light that leads and comforts, teaching you that every path He guides is filled with purpose. The same faith that carried the wise men now carries you toward everything God has promised.

When the night seemed long, the star did not fade. It burned brighter the farther they went. That is what God's light does—it grows stronger the more you trust Him. Sometimes the road seems quiet, but that silence is never empty; it is filled with His peace. You do not have to fear what you cannot see. His light is already in your heart, shining before you and behind you. The same star that led across deserts now shines in your spirit, leading you through every season with joy.

The journey of faith is never about how far you go, but who walks with you. The wise men reached Bethlehem because they followed what Heaven revealed. You will reach every promise of God because Christ Himself lives in you. You are not walking toward Him—He walks in you. Every prayer, every act of love, every moment of trust reveals His presence more and more. The journey is already blessed, because the destination lives within your heart.

When you lie down tonight, remember that your journey is not uncertain. The same Lord who lit the heavens is lighting your path. He is your beginning, your guide, and your end. Every choice made in love leads closer to His heart. The light that once led the wise men now fills your days with direction. You walk in peace, knowing His glory is your map. His promise is not far ahead—it is alive in you now.

So rest, little one, knowing your journey has already begun. You are walking in the light that cannot be lost. Christ is your path, your purpose, and your peace. The Star still shines, not above you but within you, showing that your heart already carries the way home.

Day 4: The Brightest Night

The night Jesus was born was not silent because nothing happened—it was silent because Heaven stood in awe. Angels filled the sky, but the world below was calm, wrapped in wonder. Darkness had finally met its end. The brightest light the world had ever known came quietly, in a manger. That night, the light of creation itself returned to His children. The same God who said, "Let there be light," had come to dwell among men. The heavens rejoiced, and the earth received its King. What was once a world of shadows was now touched by everlasting day.

It was the brightest night because Heaven's light did not stay above—it came down to live within. The shepherds didn't see only a baby; they saw the glory of God wrapped in love. When they heard the angel's message, they ran to see the Word made flesh. And when they looked upon Him, they saw God's heart. That same light now shines in you. Christ's glory fills your spirit so completely that no shadow can stay. The night is bright, even now, because His presence has filled the whole world.

The light that broke through Bethlehem's darkness was not a passing glow. It was eternal light—unchanging, unstoppable, and alive. When Jesus came, He did not just visit the world; He transformed it. Every heart that believes in Him becomes part of that same shining night. The world may still have storms, but His peace cannot be dimmed. You carry that peace wherever you go. You are the glow of Heaven on earth, the living proof that the brightest night never ended—it simply moved inside those who love Him.

On that night, the shepherds carried their wonder back to the fields, and everything looked different. The same hills, the same stars, the same sheep—but now everything shone with meaning. That is what Christ does in you. He turns ordinary days into holy ones, simple acts into miracles, and quiet hearts into lamps of His glory. The light of that night never left; it fills your life with the same holy brightness that filled Bethlehem. You live in the light of His finished work.

The bright night is still shining, even when your eyes close in rest. It does not depend on candles or stars. It depends on Christ, and He never fades. When you wake, the same light that filled the manger fills your morning. You walk in His brilliance, guided by His love. No darkness can return, because His life in you burns stronger than any night. You are His living flame, His bright reflection.

So rest now, child of light, and let the peace of that holy night surround you. The same angels who sang over Bethlehem still rejoice over you. The King has come, the light has risen, and the world has changed forever. The brightest night has become your everlasting day.

Day 5: The Star Above Bethlehem

High above Bethlehem, the Star shone with a light that could not be ignored. It rested over the place where the Savior lay, declaring to the heavens and to the earth that God's promise had arrived. That single light guided hearts from faraway lands to the home of divine love. Every flicker of its flame told the story of Heaven drawing near. That night, the world saw a Star—but God saw His plan fulfilled. What He had promised since the beginning now glowed above the manger, and that same light shines within your heart today.

The Star above Bethlehem was not only a signal; it was an invitation. It called the world to come and see. Wise men, shepherds, and even angels gathered around the One who would change everything. They did not need to understand all the mysteries—they simply followed the light. When you follow the peace and goodness that Christ has placed inside you, you are following the same Star. You do not need to look up at the sky to find Him. His presence already lives in you, shining brighter than the sun.

That Star never belonged to one nation or one time. It was God's declaration for all people: that light had overcome darkness forever. The glow above Bethlehem stretched across time and space to reach every heart that would believe. You are part of that eternal story. The same light that guided shepherds to the manger guides you to truth each day. Every time you listen to love, obey His Word, or forgive with joy, you walk under the same light that crowned that holy night.

Even when the world feels dim, remember that Bethlehem's Star has not gone out. The same Spirit that lit the heavens now burns gently within you. His love keeps the flame alive, turning every act of kindness into a reflection of that first glory. You are no longer standing beneath the Star—you have become its dwelling place. God has chosen your heart as His home, and His light cannot be hidden. The radiance of that night continues to shine through your life.

As you rest, imagine the Star still above your world, reminding you that Heaven's promise has not changed. Christ is near, His light never fails, and His peace covers you completely. The night that once held fear now holds glory. You are safe in the same love that filled the manger and the sky above it. The story of Bethlehem is still being told—through you.

So sleep peacefully, little one. The Star above Bethlehem shines within your spirit. Its glow will never fade, for the Light of the world has chosen you as His home. You are His brightness on the earth, the proof that His promise lives forever.

Day 6: The Gift of Sight

When the shepherds came to the manger, their eyes were opened to see what Heaven had promised. They saw more than a baby—they saw the glory of God wrapped in love. Their hearts knew they were standing in the presence of the Savior. That night was not about what their eyes could see, but what their spirits could believe. The gift of sight was not the light in the sky, but the truth revealed in their hearts. The same God who opened their eyes has opened yours, so you can see His light shining in every place, even in the quiet of your room tonight.

The gift of sight is a miracle from Heaven. It allows you to see what others may overlook—the kindness in a word, the beauty in forgiveness, the peace in a prayer. Christ gives this gift to every heart that believes. You can see with the eyes of love, seeing not what is wrong, but what God has made right. The light of Jesus helps you notice what matters most. Just as the shepherds saw the Savior, you can see His presence in your world every day.

When you look around, you will notice that light appears wherever His name is honored. The stars in the sky, the laughter of family, the warmth of love—all point to Him. The gift of sight helps you recognize that Christ is not far away. You do not have to search for Him in the distance. He has made your heart His home.

The light that once led men from afar now glows within you, giving you the vision to see through Heaven's eyes.

The shepherds left the manger with hearts full of joy because they had seen the truth with their own eyes. They returned to their flocks, but nothing looked the same again. Every day was touched by wonder. You have that same joy. When you see with the eyes of faith, every moment becomes holy. Every person becomes precious. Every day becomes a reminder that Christ is alive in you. The gift of sight changes everything because it lets you see as He sees—through perfect love.

If you ever feel surrounded by darkness, remember this: God's light never leaves your eyes. He has placed His vision in you forever. Even when the world seems dim, His brightness within you remains clear. You are not blind to His goodness; you see through it. You walk by the light that cannot fade, and your eyes are open to Heaven's truth. The gift of sight is already yours, and you will never lose it.

Now rest, little one, and close your eyes in peace. You do not need to see the star in the sky to know it still shines. Its light lives within you, glowing softly in your spirit. The same God who opened the eyes of the shepherds keeps your heart full of light tonight. You see because He has given you His sight.

Day 7: The Shining Child

The shepherds knelt before the manger and saw a child glowing with peace, though no candle burned beside Him. That light came not from the moon or the fire, but from Heaven's heart itself. The Shining Child was the promise fulfilled—God's love made visible, His mercy wrapped in skin. The night could not hold its darkness because the true Light had come. Every gaze toward that manger was a glimpse into eternity. The One who formed the stars now rested beneath them, holding the world He had made. His brightness was not distant—it was born to dwell among us forever.

This Child did not come to show light from afar; He came to place it within. Every breath He took was Heaven whispering, "I am with you." His small hands would one day touch the world with healing, His eyes would shine with perfect love, and His words would bring peace to every soul that believed. But even before He spoke, His presence was enough. The Shining Child carried all the glory of God, yet chose to live among ordinary people, proving that God's greatness shines through humility and love.

The shepherds could not contain their joy. They ran through the fields shouting the good news: "The Savior is born!" The light they saw in the Child now burned in them. That is what happens when you see Him—you shine too. Christ does not give you a borrowed light; He shares His very own. The glow that filled the manger now fills your heart. Every smile, every act of kindness, every moment of faith reveals the same light the shepherds saw that night.

Even now, the world still searches for that brightness. Many look to the sky, but the true Star shines through you. You are the reflection of the Shining Child, the proof that God has come near. When you love others, you reveal His presence. When you forgive, you release His peace. The more you believe, the brighter your life becomes. His light does not fade—it multiplies. You are His lamp in the world, carrying His warmth wherever you go.

When you close your eyes tonight, imagine that little manger glowing with love. That same light surrounds you even now. It covers your room, your dreams, and your heart. The Shining Child has not grown dim; He has simply moved His home from the stable to your spirit. The world may sleep, but His glory does not rest. His light burns quietly inside you, making you part of the story that began in Bethlehem.

Sleep now, beloved one, under the same light that filled that holy night. The Shining Child is your peace, your joy, your everlasting light. He has made His home in you, and His brightness will never end.

Day 8: The Shepherd's Light

The night the angels sang, the shepherds were the first to hear the good news. They were watching their sheep under the same stars that glowed above Bethlehem, unaware that Heaven was about to visit them. Suddenly, light filled the fields—a light not of earth, but of God. The angels told them, "Unto you is born this day in the city of David a Saviour." The shepherds saw the sky blaze with glory, and they knew it was real. That same light that shone upon them still shines upon you, for the same Savior who came that night lives within your heart.

The shepherds were not rich or famous, yet God chose them to see His glory first. That is how God's love works—it reaches for the humble, the quiet, and the willing. You do not have to be perfect or powerful for His light to shine through you. Christ came for every heart that listens. The shepherds did not earn His favor; they simply received it. And tonight, you rest in that same grace. His light is not given by measure; it fills every believer completely.

When the angels returned to Heaven, the light did not fade from the shepherds' hearts. They ran to the manger, guided by faith and joy. Every step they took glowed with purpose. When they found the Child, they knelt and worshipped, knowing they were standing in the presence of God. You, too, walk in that same light each day. You carry the same message they carried back to the fields—that Christ is born, that peace is here, that God is with us. You shine because His Spirit shines through you.

The Shepherd's Light reminds you that God's presence is not far away. He is with you in your daily life—at home, at school, in every quiet moment. You do not need to see angels to know He is near. The same peace that surrounded the shepherds surrounds you. The same joy that filled their hearts fills yours. Every time you speak love, you become part of their story—the ones who saw the glory and could not keep silent.

Even when nights seem long or silent, the Shepherd's Light still shines. His peace watches over you like those shepherds watched over their flocks. You are safe under His care, guarded by His everlasting light. The Savior who came for them has already come for you. You are loved with the same love that broke through the sky. The Light of the world is your Shepherd, and His brightness will never fade from your life.

Now rest, little one, under His gentle light. The same glow that filled the fields of Bethlehem now fills your heart. The Shepherd's Light guides you, comforts you, and keeps you. Sleep in His peace, knowing that you are always in His care. His light shines through you, and it will never grow dim.

Day 9: The Light in the Stable

The stable was quiet, filled only with the sounds of gentle animals breathing and the soft cries of the newborn King. It was not a palace, but Heaven's glory filled it completely. The walls of wood and stone glowed with the light that no flame could make. That stable became the center of creation's joy because Christ, the Light of the world, had entered it. The place that seemed ordinary became holy because God's presence had made His home there. And just as that small room shone that night, your heart shines now—because His light has chosen you as its dwelling.

The Light in the Stable showed that God's glory is not found in riches or fame but in love. The King of Heaven came to earth with no crown but kindness, no robe but humility. He did not need a throne to show His power; He needed only His love. That love now fills your life. When you speak peace, you shine like that stable. When you forgive, you open the door for His glory to shine through. The Light that made that night bright now glows through every believer who welcomes Him.

The animals in the stable rested quietly beside the manger, unaware that they were near the Creator who had made them. Even the straw beneath Him held Heaven's secret. It reminds you that God's presence fills ordinary places. Wherever you are, He is there.

You do not have to go far to find His light; it shines where you love, where you believe, and where you rest in Him. The stable was not chosen for its beauty—it was chosen for its humility, and so is your heart.

The light that filled that small space did not stay there. It spread across fields, across nations, across time, reaching even you. The Light in the Stable has never gone out. Every song of praise, every kind word, every prayer of faith keeps it glowing. You are part of that eternal story—the child of God who carries His brightness into the world. The same light that warmed the stable warms your heart, and no night can overcome it.

If you ever wonder where God's glory is, remember the manger. The world expected greatness, but Heaven came in simplicity. That same light comes to you daily, quiet but unstoppable. It shines in your joy, your laughter, your kindness, and your courage. The Light in the Stable was not just for that night—it was the beginning of light for every heart forever.

Rest now, knowing that your heart is His stable. Christ has made His home in you, and His light fills every corner. The same glow that brightened that humble room shines from within you now. Sleep in peace, child of the Light. Heaven's glory has come to stay.

Day 10: The Glow of Obedience

When the angel spoke to Mary, she answered, "Be it unto me according to thy word." In that moment, her obedience became the doorway for Heaven's light to enter the world. She did not wait to see how everything would unfold—she simply believed. The glow of her obedience was brighter than any star. God's light always follows believing hearts. Every "yes" you give to His truth becomes a spark that shines in the dark. Obedience is not a heavy burden; it is the quiet joy of walking in step with His love, knowing that His way always brings peace.

The shepherds obeyed when the angel told them to go, and their obedience led them straight to the Savior. They could have stayed in their fields, but they chose to move when Heaven spoke. Because of that, they saw the glory that changed everything. You, too, carry that same choice each day—to follow the light or stay in the shadows. When you listen to God's voice and walk in His Word, your heart glows with His presence. His joy follows obedience like dawn follows night.

The glow of obedience is gentle but strong. It cannot be forced or faked; it comes from love. When you choose kindness over anger, truth over fear, and forgiveness over pride, your light grows brighter. The world may not always notice, but Heaven sees. Every small act of obedience is like another star lit in the sky. You were made to shine with that glow—not because you have to, but because His Spirit in you makes it your nature to do good. His light has already given you the power to walk in truth.

When Joseph obeyed the angel and took Mary and the baby to safety, he proved that love listens. Obedience is not about rules; it's about trust. Joseph trusted God even when he didn't understand the full plan. His obedience protected the Light of the world. And now, Christ in you leads you with that same faith. You do not have to understand everything to follow Him. You only need to believe that His path is always filled with life. When you do, His glow surrounds your steps, and peace fills every moment.

Even when it's hard, obedience keeps the light shining. It may not always be easy to do what's right, but every time you say "yes" to truth, darkness loses ground. God's light grows stronger in you because obedience opens the door for His glory to move freely. The glow you carry is not your own; it is His reflection. As you trust and follow Him, your life becomes a lamp others can see from afar, guiding them to Christ's love.

Now rest in peace, knowing that your obedience has made room for His light. The same glow that surrounded Mary, Joseph, and the shepherds shines in you tonight. The Glow of Obedience is your gift to the world—proof that God's Word is alive in you. Sleep beneath His brightness, for His light will never leave you.

Day 11: The Guiding Star

The Star that led the wise men did not move by accident. Every shimmer, every pause, every path it traced in the sky was directed by God. It was a guiding light, steady and true, leading hearts toward the Savior. In the same way, Christ's light within you is never uncertain. It does not wander or dim. His Spirit guides every step, showing you where to go, when to rest, and how to walk in love. The Guiding Star reminds you that God never leaves you to find the way alone. His presence leads you gently, shining the path of peace before your feet.

The wise men did not follow their feelings—they followed the light. They trusted that the One who called them would lead them safely. Each night, the Star appeared again, reminding them that Heaven was still with them. You can rest in that same assurance. Whether the way seems clear or hidden, the Light of Christ in you never fails. You do not have to fear missing the path, because the One who guides you lives inside your heart. His direction is not far off in the distance; it is the still, steady glow that fills your spirit with peace.

The Guiding Star teaches you that faith is not about knowing every turn, but trusting every moment. Sometimes God's light shines just enough for the next step, not the whole journey. That's how He keeps your heart close to His. The wise men learned that the path of obedience is illuminated one step at a time. You, too, walk under that same grace. Christ in you shines brighter than any star above you, showing that every road walked in love will lead to joy. His presence is your direction, His peace your compass.

Even when clouds cover the sky, the Star still shines. You may not always see it, but its light is never gone. The same is true of God's guidance. There will be days when you cannot see the full picture, but you can trust the One who holds it. The Guiding Star never failed the wise men, and God's Spirit will never fail you. His Word remains the light for your path, a lamp to your feet, a steady glow in every season. The light that once led kings now leads your heart every day.

When the wise men finally reached the place where Jesus lay, their long journey ended in joy. Every mile, every desert, every night of travel was worth it. The same is true for you. Every time you follow the light, every time you trust His leading, you discover His presence waiting for you. The Guiding Star does not only point to where you are going—it reveals Who walks beside you.

Now rest, little one, beneath His gentle glow. The Guiding Star that shone over Bethlehem now shines over your life. Christ Himself is your light, your map, and your guide. His brightness surrounds your dreams tonight, leading you always in love.

Day 12: The Wise Men's Path

The wise men saw the Star and knew it meant something greater than themselves. They left their homes, their comfort, and their routines to follow its light. They didn't travel in certainty—they traveled in faith. Every step brought them closer to the promise God had placed in their hearts. The same Spirit that guided them guides you. You may not see the whole journey ahead, but the light of Christ in you is enough for every step. The Wise Men's Path is the walk of trust —following love, believing truth, and moving forward when God's peace shines in your heart.

The wise men carried gifts, but before they offered them, they offered their hearts. Their journey was an act of worship. They followed not for reward, but for revelation. The closer they came to the Light, the more their hearts were filled with wonder. You walk the same kind of road each day. When you obey, forgive, and love others, you bring gifts to the King. Your worship is not just in words—it is in every choice to follow His truth. The Wise Men's Path is not measured in miles, but in love that grows brighter the nearer you walk with Him.

Their path was long and sometimes hard, but the Star never left them. It went before them through every valley and over every hill. That's how Christ leads you —faithfully, patiently, step by step. You never walk alone. The same light that filled the sky above them now fills your heart. Even when you don't understand the road ahead, His peace tells you you're going the right way. The Wise Men's Path is the journey of every believer—guided by unseen hands, strengthened by unending light.

When the wise men finally saw the child, their hearts overflowed. They bowed low, not before a throne but before a manger. In that moment, they realized that greatness had been born in humility. The world seeks glory in high places, but God reveals it in love. You, too, find your greatest joy not in being seen, but in seeing Him. The Wise Men's Path leads not to pride but to worship—to bowing before Christ and giving all that you are to Him.

When they returned home, they were not the same. The journey had changed them. Every mile walked in faith left Heaven's imprint on their hearts. That is what happens to you when you follow His light—you are transformed by every step. The more you walk in love, the more you reflect His glory. The Wise Men's Path never really ends, for it leads from faith to faith, from light to light, until all that remains is His everlasting peace.

Now rest, little one, knowing your path is sure. The same Star that led the wise men still shines within you. Christ, your Light, your Guide, your King, walks with you always. The Wise Men's Path has become your own, and every step you take glows with Heaven's joy.

Day 13: The Treasure of Light

When the wise men entered the house where Jesus was, they fell to their knees in awe. Before them was the Treasure of Heaven, wrapped in the simplicity of a child. They opened their gifts of gold, frankincense, and myrrh, but none of those compared to what they received in return—the light of His presence. In that moment, they found more than they had ever sought. Every gift they brought was a reflection of what Christ would later give to all: purity, kingship, and life everlasting. The Treasure of Light is not found in gold or silver, but in knowing that God Himself has chosen to dwell within you.

The light that filled the room that day did not fade when they left. It became part of their hearts. They had seen the King, and they could never forget His face. That is what happens when you encounter Christ. His light becomes your treasure—something that can never be stolen, lost, or dimmed. Every time you remember His love, every time you walk in His truth, that treasure grows brighter. You carry the same radiance they saw, for His Spirit has made you the keeper of His glory.

The Treasure of Light is not meant to be hidden. It shines through kindness, forgiveness, and joy. When you share love, you share Him. The world may look for treasure in what can be touched or owned, but your greatest riches are unseen. Christ has placed His light in your heart as a gift for the world to see. The same light that lit the sky over Bethlehem now glows through your words and actions. You are His lamp, His vessel of glory, carrying Heaven's treasure into the earth.

When you feel small or unimportant, remember the wise men knelt before a child in a humble home. The greatest treasure was hidden in simplicity. God's power is revealed the same way in you. You do not need to be great in the world's eyes to shine brightly. Every quiet act of faith, every gentle word of love releases His light. The Treasure of Light is not something you earn—it is who you have become in Him. His glory lives in you because His presence has made you His own.

When night falls, the stars still shine, but the true treasure remains in hearts that believe. You are not empty-handed before God. You carry the most precious gift of all—Christ Himself living within you. His light fills every part of your life, turning ordinary moments into holy ones. The same treasure that made the wise men rejoice now makes your spirit shine. You have found what the whole world seeks—God with us, God in you, the everlasting Light.

So rest, beloved child, holding your treasure close. The light that guided the wise men rests within you now. The Treasure of Light is yours forever, shining through your life for all to see. Heaven's richest gift has already been given, and His glory will never fade.

Day 14: The Lamp of Peace

The night Jesus was born, Heaven sang of peace on earth, goodwill toward men. That song was more than music—it was a promise fulfilled. The Lamp of Peace had been lit in a world that knew only darkness. From that moment on, true peace was no longer something to search for—it had come to live among us. Christ is that peace. He does not simply bring calm; He *is* calm. His presence quiets every storm, silences every fear, and fills every heart that believes. When you rest in Him, His peace lights your path like a lamp that never burns out.

The peace of God is not fragile. It is steady, unshaken by what happens around you. The same peace that kept the manger still while angels rejoiced is alive in you now. It does not depend on noise or silence, success or comfort—it comes from knowing that Christ has already won every battle. The Lamp of Peace glows within your spirit, reminding you that nothing can separate you from His love. The world may shake, but your heart remains still, anchored in His unchanging Word.

The shepherds felt that peace as they looked upon the sleeping Savior. The air itself seemed holy. Every sound was gentle because Heaven's rest had come to earth. That peace is yours tonight. You do not have to chase it or wait for it—it already lives in you. When you choose to forgive, when you speak with kindness, when you trust God even in uncertainty, His lamp shines brighter. Peace is not a dream—it is your reality because Christ has made His home within you.

Sometimes, the world tries to steal your calm, but it cannot touch what God has given. His peace does not flicker when trouble comes; it grows stronger. It lights every dark place and guards your mind from fear. You are not left in confusion or worry, for the Light of Christ has conquered both. The Lamp of Peace burns quietly, always reminding you that God's love never fades. Even when life feels rushed or loud, His calm remains unbroken, like a steady flame in a gentle hand.

The same light that filled that stable fills your heart tonight. The peace that rested over the manger now rests over you. It does not matter where you are or what the day has held—His peace is enough. It covers you like soft light over still waters. You can breathe, knowing that Heaven's calm surrounds your thoughts and keeps your dreams safe in His care. The Lamp of Peace glows through every heartbeat, whispering that you belong to Him.

So close your eyes, beloved child, and rest in His light. The Lamp of Peace burns in you forever, never fading, never growing dim. The same peace that filled Bethlehem fills your room tonight. The Savior who calmed the world's storm has already calmed your heart. Sleep under His peace, wrapped in His everlasting light.

Day 15: The Star Over Every Home

The night the Star stood still over Bethlehem, Heaven declared that love had found its home on earth. The same light that rested above the stable shines now over every home that welcomes Christ. The Star was not a decoration—it was a declaration that God had come to dwell with His people. Wherever hearts believe, the light rests. Your home, no matter how small or quiet, becomes holy ground when filled with His presence. The Star over Bethlehem has not vanished; it has multiplied, shining above and within every home where Christ is adored.

When families gather in love, Heaven draws near. Every word spoken with kindness, every prayer whispered in faith, keeps the Star shining. God's light does not visit for a season—it stays. Just as the Star hovered over the place where Jesus lay, His Spirit hovers over you now. He watches over your home with peace that cannot be shaken. You may not see the light with your eyes, but Heaven sees it glowing—because His presence fills your rooms with warmth and safety. Christ's light has made your home His dwelling.

The Star over every home means no family is forgotten. God's light finds every door, every heart, every child who believes. The same love that filled the manger fills your table. The same glory that guided the shepherds watches your steps. You live under Heaven's light—not just outside your walls but within them. Wherever you pray, forgive, or sing His name, the Star shines brighter. Your home becomes a reflection of that first night in Bethlehem—a place where peace reigns and love never ends.

Even when the world feels dark, the Star over your home does not fade. It shines through patience, through laughter, through faith that endures. The light reminds you that Christ's presence is not fragile or far away—it is constant and close. He fills your house with grace the same way He filled the stable with glory. The promise that began in Bethlehem continues every day you welcome Him. You do not live beneath shadows; you live beneath His light.

When you look at the stars above, remember that Heaven watches you with joy. God does not see empty rooms—He sees homes glowing with His Spirit. The Star above Bethlehem was the first spark of a world forever changed, and that change still shines through families like yours. The Star over every home is the proof that love wins, that peace remains, that God lives with us. His light fills your walls, your heart, and your life.

Now rest, little one, beneath the Star that never fades. Its light covers your home and fills your dreams. The same glory that hovered over the manger now hovers over you. The Star over every home shines within your spirit, whispering that Christ has made your life His dwelling place. Sleep in His peace—He is here, and His light will never go out.

Day 16: The Night Heaven Rejoiced

The night Christ was born, Heaven could not stay silent. Angels filled the sky, their voices bursting with joy that had waited since the beginning of time. "Glory to God in the highest," they sang, "and on earth peace, goodwill toward men." That night was not just the birth of a child—it was the birth of redemption, the unveiling of love in its purest form. Heaven rejoiced because the plan of God was complete. The Savior had come, and light had returned to the world. Every angel's song was a celebration that God's promise had finally taken form in the heart of His creation.

Heaven rejoiced not only because Christ was born, but because now humanity could live in His light. The angels saw what people had longed to see—God with us. Their song echoed across the fields, and that echo still fills the earth today. When you worship, when you speak truth, when you show kindness, Heaven rejoices again. The same joy that rang through the stars that night fills your spirit now. You are part of Heaven's song, because Christ lives in you. The night Heaven rejoiced has become your eternal day.

The shepherds stood beneath that shining sky, unable to move for wonder. The brilliance of Heaven surrounded them, yet it did not frighten them—it comforted them.

They heard the good news: "A Savior is born." That same message still speaks to you. God has not left the world in darkness. He has come and made His home within you. Heaven's joy now fills your heart, for you are living proof of God's love fulfilled. The song that once filled the fields now fills your soul.

Heaven's rejoicing was not for angels alone—it was for you. Each note of their song was a message of peace meant for every heart that would believe. You do not need to look to the sky to hear it; it plays quietly in your spirit. Every time you choose love over anger, or faith over fear, that song grows louder. Heaven rejoices because Christ's life shines through you. You are the reason light still fills the earth, for His joy has made you its carrier.

The night Heaven rejoiced did not end when morning came—it continues through every life touched by His light. The angels' joy has not faded; it has multiplied. Every believer is part of their chorus now, living as proof that God's promise is true. The heavens still watch with delight as you walk in His peace and shine His glory. You are part of the same celebration that began over Bethlehem, for the same King reigns in your heart.

Now rest, beloved one, under Heaven's song. The same joy that filled the sky fills your room tonight. The angels still rejoice because the Light of the world lives in you. Sleep in that peace, wrapped in the music of Heaven's love—a love that will never end.

Day 17: The Morning Dawned

As the first light of morning touched Bethlehem, a new day began unlike any other. The world that had slept in darkness awoke to the brightness of grace. The same sun that rose over the stable shone upon a new creation. The Savior had come, and nothing would ever be the same. The Morning Dawned with the warmth of God's love spilling over the earth, reaching every heart that would believe. The shadows that once covered the world faded away, for the true Light had risen. That morning still shines through time—it shines through you.

When Christ came, Heaven's light met the earth forever. The dawn was not just a moment in time—it was a promise fulfilled. The Light of the world had conquered the night once and for all. The same Spirit that lit that dawn burns within your heart. Every morning you awaken is a reminder that darkness no longer rules you. The morning of His mercy has no end. You live in the brightness of redemption, and the same joy that filled the sky that day fills your life even now.

The Morning Dawned with peace, because the curse of sin had met its answer. God's love had stepped into the story. The cry of a newborn King had silenced the enemy's hold forever. You no longer live waiting for freedom—it has already come. The morning that rose in Bethlehem continues in your spirit. Every step you take is touched by that light. Every breath you draw glows with the grace He gave. You are a child of the dawn, a living witness that Christ's victory has already made all things new.

The dawn of Christ's coming changed not only the world but the hearts of those who believe. The shepherds returned to their fields filled with light, their lives forever brightened by what they had seen. You walk in that same glow. No matter how long the night seems, the morning has already come. God's mercy is new each day because His presence is constant. The Morning Dawned not as an event but as a Person—and that Person lives within you.

Even now, the world still turns toward the light, just as hearts turn toward Christ. Every sunrise is a whisper of His glory, every beam a reminder that the night cannot last. You do not wait for hope—it rises in you daily. You are already standing in the light of His love. The morning of salvation has come, and its glow will never fade. The same Lord who rose that day keeps your spirit awake in His brightness forever.

Now rest, precious one, beneath the peace of His endless morning. The light that filled Bethlehem's dawn fills your room tonight. Though the world sleeps, Heaven's brightness remains. The Morning Dawned once for all, and its warmth will never leave you. Sleep in that light—the dawn has come, and you are already shining in it.

Day 18: The Light Within

The same light that broke through the darkness of Bethlehem now lives inside your heart. The Light Within is not a borrowed glow—it is Christ Himself. He does not visit and then leave; He abides forever. When you believe in Him, His Spirit becomes your flame, steady and pure. The same glory that shone over shepherds and kings now shines from within you. You are not waiting for more light; you already carry all that Heaven can give. The child in the manger has become the King within your heart, and His light cannot be hidden.

The Light Within never flickers or fades. It does not depend on what you feel or see. It is constant because Christ is constant. When you speak truth, forgive others, or choose love, that light shines brighter. It is Heaven's way of showing the world that God's promise has been fulfilled. The darkness may try to whisper, but it cannot overcome the light. You are filled with the same brilliance that filled the night when angels sang. The Light Within you is eternal—it burns with the power of His love.

Every believer carries this glow, whether in laughter or in tears. The Light Within gives strength in quiet moments and courage in every trial. You may not always notice it, but others see it when you live in peace. It is the reflection of Christ Himself shining through your life. The same fire that guided Israel, the same glory that filled the stable, burns in you now. You are His living lantern in the world, showing that His light has conquered the night forever.

The Light Within does more than guide you—it transforms you. It changes fear into faith, sorrow into hope, and doubt into certainty. It reminds you that you are never alone. Even when the world seems dark, that glow remains unbroken. It shines in your words, your thoughts, your love. The same presence that once filled the temple now fills your heart. The true miracle of Christmas is not only that Christ came near, but that He chose to live inside you.

The light you carry is not small—it is divine. It is the same Spirit that raised Jesus from the dead, the same fire that ignited creation. You do not carry a spark—you carry the flame of Heaven. And that flame is your identity. You walk in it, speak from it, and rest in it. Nothing can put it out, because it is not of this world. You are lit from the inside by the One who is light itself.

Now rest, child of glory. The Light Within warms you even as you sleep. The same flame that burned over Bethlehem now burns in your soul. You do not need to chase the light—it already lives in you. Sleep in peace, knowing that Christ's brightness fills every part of your life, and His light within you will never fade.

Day 19: The World Made Bright

When Christ entered the world, He did not just light one night—He lit all of time. The world that once groaned under darkness now shines with His glory. Every heart that believes becomes a lamp of His love. The World Made Bright is not a faraway dream; it is the reality of His presence filling every place. When you walk in peace, when you speak truth, when you love as He loves, the world around you glows with His brightness. You carry the same light that transformed Bethlehem into Heaven's doorway. Through you, His light continues to spread until the whole world sees His glory.

The light of Christ changes everything it touches. It turns fear into faith and sorrow into song. The same power that broke through the sky that holy night is alive in you now. You are not waiting for the world to brighten; it already has, because Christ lives in His people. Each word of kindness, each act of grace, shines like a star in the dark. The world may not understand it, but it cannot ignore it. His light in you is unstoppable, and it is making all things new.

When Jesus walked the earth, every step He took brought healing, joy, and life. Now He walks in you, bringing that same light to others. You are His living testimony that darkness has lost. The world made bright begins wherever love is shown, wherever mercy speaks, wherever forgiveness reigns. Every time you choose His way, you reveal the dawn that never ends. The Star that once shone above Bethlehem now shines through your eyes, your smile, and your life. You are part of the brightness that fills the world with hope.

The light does not fade when days grow difficult. It shines even stronger in adversity, proving that nothing can extinguish God's presence. The world is not too dark for His glory—it is the very canvas for His brilliance. You were made to shine, even in the storm, because His peace anchors you. Every challenge becomes a stage for His light to appear. The World Made Bright is not only around you—it is within you, and it spreads wherever you go.

The angels rejoiced because they saw what you now live—the Kingdom of Heaven on earth. Their song still echoes: "Glory to God in the highest." You are the continuation of that praise. Your light joins Heaven's chorus, declaring that Christ has come and reigns forever. The world is bright because His life has filled it. The same power that spoke light into creation now speaks through your heart.

Now rest, beloved one, in the brightness of His love. The world around you glows with His peace, and the world within you burns with His Spirit. The World Made Bright is not only history—it is your present reality. Sleep beneath His shining grace, knowing that His light through you keeps the world aglow forever.

Day 20: The Glow That Guides

When the wise men followed the Star, they did not know how long the journey would take, yet they trusted the light before them. The same kind of glow now guides your heart each day. The Glow That Guides is Christ's own Spirit leading you through every moment of life. You do not wander aimlessly; His presence is your direction. Even when the road seems uncertain, His peace confirms the way. Just as the Star never failed those who followed it, His Word never fails those who believe. The glow that led them to the Savior now lives within you, quietly leading you in paths of truth and love.

The Word of God is your lamp and your light. It shows you where to walk, even when everything else seems dark. You are never without direction, for His Spirit inside you knows every turn. When you listen to His Word and trust His promises, the Glow That Guides grows brighter. It shines through patience, through kindness, and through faith that refuses to quit. Each step you take in obedience becomes another spark of His light in the world. You walk in safety because you walk in Him.

The glow that guides is not loud or flashing—it is steady and sure. It speaks through peace, not panic. When your heart feels calm and full of quiet assurance, that is His light leading you. You do not need to chase signs or wait for stars to appear in the sky; the same Light that led the wise men burns in your spirit. His guidance does not come from outside but from within. Every decision made in love, every thought aligned with truth, follows His glow perfectly.

The world tries to lead with noise and fear, but the Spirit of Christ leads with peace. His glow does not confuse or rush—it rests and reassures. You will never lose your way when you keep your eyes on Him. Even if the path bends or slows, His light remains constant. The Glow That Guides does not fade when life feels difficult; it shines even more clearly, reminding you that you are safe in His will. Every step in faith reveals more of His glory.

The same God who led Israel by a pillar of fire and who guided the wise men by a Star now guides you by His Spirit. You are never left alone. His light is your compass, His peace your confirmation, His Word your steady flame. Wherever you go, His glow goes with you, lighting the way for others to see. Your life becomes a living signpost, pointing the world to Jesus —the Light of all mankind.

So rest tonight in peace, child of light. The Glow That Guides will not go out. It watches over your dreams and keeps your path bright. You are surrounded by the same light that filled Bethlehem's sky. Sleep knowing that His Word, His peace, and His Spirit will guide you forever.

Day 21: The Eternal Flame

Long before the world began, God's light already burned bright. His love had no beginning and will have no end. When Christ came, that unending flame took form in a manger so that His light could live within us forever. The Eternal Flame is not a fire that flickers with time—it is everlasting. It shines through eternity and fills every heart that believes. The same light that broke the darkness on that holy night still burns in you now. It never fades, never weakens, never sleeps. The life of Christ in you is eternal, steady as the sunrise, and bright as the promise of Heaven itself.

This flame is not made of earthly fire. It cannot be put out by sorrow, fear, or death. It is the fire of divine love—the very presence of God's Spirit. The Eternal Flame burns within your heart, reminding you that His Word is unchanging and His truth is forever. It glows in worship, it shines in stillness, and it warms every soul that draws near to it. The world may grow cold, but His flame in you never will. Christ has joined His life to yours, and that union cannot be undone.

The Eternal Flame lights the way through every season. When days feel joyful, it shines in your laughter. When nights feel long, it glows in your faith. Nothing can dim its light because it comes from Heaven's heart. The same love that sent angels to sing now lives through your voice, your hands, and your life. You are not a candle waiting to be lit—you are already burning with the fire of God's Spirit. The flame in you carries His warmth wherever you go, touching hearts that long for His peace.

Even when you face challenges, the flame never leaves. It does not depend on how strong you feel—it depends on how faithful He is. The Eternal Flame is the promise that God will never abandon His children. It is the light of Christ's victory, glowing in every believer. You are surrounded and filled by the same presence that once filled the stable. His love burns with patience, His peace with power, His joy with endless strength. That is the fire that makes you alive.

This flame is your forever light. It will shine in your heart on earth and glow even brighter in eternity. The same Spirit who raised Jesus from the dead lives in you and will never depart. The Eternal Flame is your reminder that you belong to a Kingdom that never ends. You are lit from within by the life of God Himself. His fire in you is not a moment—it is forever.

Now rest, child of everlasting light. The Eternal Flame watches over you, glowing softly as you sleep. The same love that began before time began will still be shining when all else fades. You are wrapped in its warmth, safe in its glow, and alive in its promise. The Eternal Flame burns within you always.

Day 22: The Star in Your Eyes

When people looked upon the Star of Bethlehem, they saw the glory of God shining across the sky. That same glory now shines in your eyes. The Star in Your Eyes is the reflection of Christ within you—the proof that His light has made your heart His home. When you look with love, Heaven looks through you. When you forgive, mercy gleams in your gaze. The same light that guided wise men and comforted shepherds glows now from your spirit. You are not trying to find the light; you are already shining with it. The Star that once marked His coming now lives in you, and the world sees Him through your eyes.

Your eyes were made to shine with kindness and truth. The peace of Christ rests behind them, bright as the morning. When you smile, Heaven's warmth touches the world. When you look at others with compassion, you reveal the heart of God. The Star in Your Eyes is not for decoration—it is for direction. Through you, others find hope, comfort, and faith. Every gentle glance, every moment of understanding, points people toward the love that never fails. Christ's light through you makes the world brighter every day.

The reflection of Christ cannot be hidden. Even when you feel small or unnoticed, His light still shines through you. The glow in your eyes is the same power that conquered the grave. It is not pride that makes you bright—it is His presence. You do not shine because of what you have done, but because of who lives in you. When the world grows cold, one look of love from you can melt hearts. The Star in Your Eyes reminds the earth that the Savior still lives, still loves, and still reigns through His people.

Each time you look at creation with wonder, Heaven smiles. Each time you see someone with grace, God's light grows stronger in the world. The Star in Your Eyes is the evidence that darkness has lost. It cannot win where His light has taken root. Even when tears fill your eyes, His glow remains—unchanged, unbroken, unstoppable. The world may not understand what it sees, but Heaven knows that your gaze carries the presence of the King.

Your eyes are the windows of His glory. They carry both the memory of the manger and the promise of eternity. The same eyes that see stars above also see the light within. Every time you look in faith, you see what Heaven sees—Christ alive in you. The Star in Your Eyes is more than a reflection; it is the proof of God's victory made visible. You are the living reminder that Emmanuel has come, and His light has no end.

Now rest, little one, beneath His watchful glow. The Star in Your Eyes still shines even as you sleep. Its brightness guards your dreams and fills your heart with peace. Christ's light never leaves you—it shines

through you forever. Sleep knowing that Heaven sees
its reflection in you.

Day 23: The Light That Leads

From the moment the Star appeared, it had one purpose —to lead. It did not shine for itself; it shone to reveal the way to Jesus. That same light now lives in you, and it still leads hearts home. The Light That Leads is the presence of Christ guiding you from within, showing you the path of love, peace, and truth. You do not wander in confusion because the One who is the Way walks inside you. His light does not flicker or fade. It goes before you in wisdom and follows behind you in mercy, keeping your steps sure and steady.

Every time you listen to His Word, the light grows brighter. The Scriptures are not just words—they are the voice of the One who leads you. "Thy word is a lamp unto my feet, and a light unto my path." His truth keeps you from stumbling and helps you walk in peace. You never have to guess where He is leading because love always points the way. The Light That Leads never contradicts His goodness. It is gentle but strong, clear but patient, and always draws you closer to Him.

The world often tries to lead with fear, but Christ leads with peace. His light does not push—it invites. It does not demand—it guides. You can trust the glow in your heart that says, "This is the way; walk in it." The same Spirit that led Mary and Joseph, that guided the shepherds, and that drew the wise men still leads you today. He knows every step before you take it, every need before you ask, every answer before you pray. His leading is never wrong because His light is perfect.

The Light That Leads not only guides you but also shines through you to guide others. When you walk in truth, others see the path. When you forgive, others learn peace. When you speak kindness, others find courage. Christ's light in you becomes a compass for those searching in the dark. You are a lamp in His hands, helping the world find its way home. You do not have to try to shine—it happens naturally when His Spirit fills you.

Even in moments of uncertainty, His light remains steady. You may not see the end of the road, but He does. The Light That Leads never stops at the edge of what you understand; it carries you safely through every unknown. You can rest in His direction because His path always ends in joy. The same Star that led to the manger now leads your heart daily, one peaceful step at a time.

Now rest, beloved one, beneath His guiding glow. The Light That Leads watches over your dreams and prepares your morning. You are safe in His care, secure in His love, and surrounded by His light. Sleep knowing that His way is sure and that His presence will lead you forever.

Day 24: The Night Before the Miracle

Before the miracle of Christ's birth, there was silence. The world slept under a blanket of waiting, unaware that Heaven was about to touch the earth. The Night Before the Miracle was not filled with noise or crowds, but with quiet expectation. God's promise was ready to appear. Even when the world seemed still, His plan was already in motion. That is how His love works—it shines before you even see it. The same peace that covered Bethlehem that night now rests on you. When everything seems quiet, it is not emptiness; it is the stillness before His glory appears again.

Mary and Joseph rested in faith that night. They had no room in the inn, no comfort except God's promise. Yet their hearts were full of peace. They trusted that what God said would come to pass. The world outside did not see what Heaven saw—a miracle ready to be born. In the same way, God's light often moves quietly within you. You may not see what He is doing, but His purpose is unfolding. The night before the miracle is always calm, because peace comes before light breaks forth.

That holy night reminds you that God never forgets His word. Even when the world is dark, His plan is already shining behind the scenes. Every moment of waiting is filled with His presence. You may not hear angels singing yet, but they are near. You may not see the light yet, but it is already rising. The Night Before the Miracle teaches you to rest in faith, not in sight. God's promises are never late. They arrive exactly when His glory will be most seen.

The shepherds were watching their flocks, unaware that Heaven's plan would soon unfold before their eyes. They didn't realize they were standing on holy ground. In the same way, your ordinary days are full of extraordinary grace. The quiet moments before the miracle are the places where faith grows deepest. The waiting is never wasted, for His light is already forming, ready to break through your horizon with joy.

When you feel stillness in your heart, it may be God preparing something beautiful. His peace always comes first, wrapping you like the gentle calm before dawn. The night before the miracle is the time to breathe, to trust, to rest. God's promises are sure, and His timing is perfect. Just as that silent night gave birth to the Light of the world, every promise He has planted in you will shine in its season.

Now rest, little one, in the peace of that holy night. The same quiet that covered Bethlehem covers you. Heaven is never late. The miracle is already near, and its light is already yours. Sleep in stillness and trust, for the night before the miracle is only the beginning of joy everlasting.

Day 25: The Day Heaven Came Down

The morning light touched the earth, and Heaven's promise became real. The Day Heaven Came Down was the day love took form, grace became visible, and peace began to live among men. In a small stable, beneath the Star of glory, God Himself stepped into time. Heaven did not send an army or thunder from the sky—it sent a child. That day changed everything. The distance between God and His children vanished forever. Heaven came down, not in might, but in mercy. The same Christ who was born in Bethlehem now lives within you, proving that Heaven still walks the earth through every heart that believes.

Angels filled the sky that morning because joy could no longer be contained. They sang not of judgment but of peace. The curse was broken, and light had returned to the world. Every song they sang declared that God's heart had come home to His creation. That song still echoes through your spirit. When you speak words of love, you join the same heavenly chorus. When you forgive, when you bless, when you lift others, Heaven sings through you. The Day Heaven Came Down is not just history—it is your reality every time you reveal Christ's love.

Mary held the Savior in her arms, but what she held was more than a baby—it was eternity wrapped in time. The same presence that formed galaxies now rested against her heart. That is what God has done for you. He has placed His presence within your heart, closer than breath, nearer than thought. You do not have to reach for Heaven; Heaven has already reached for you. The Day Heaven Came Down was not the end of the story—it was the beginning of life as God intended, where His Spirit and yours live as one.

The shepherds ran from the fields to see the miracle with their own eyes. What they found was simple—a child lying in a manger—but that simplicity held all the power of creation. God chose humility to reveal His glory. Even now, He chooses simple hearts to carry His light. You are part of that same miracle. When you love purely, when you speak truthfully, when you walk humbly, Heaven shines through you. Every act of grace is another glimpse of that day when glory first touched the ground.

The Day Heaven Came Down is the proof that God's love has no boundaries. He came not to visit, but to dwell. He did not send light from afar; He became the Light among us. And now, He has made His home inside you. You carry Heaven's glow wherever you go. The same power that lit the sky over Bethlehem fills your spirit with unending peace.

Rest now, beloved one, beneath Heaven's gentle glow. The day that changed the world still changes hearts today. Heaven has not left—it lives in you. Sleep in peace, knowing that the same light that came down now rises within you forever.

Day 26: The Shining Kingdom

When Christ was born, a new Kingdom entered the world—not built by hands, not ruled by fear, but shining with love that never ends. The Shining Kingdom is the reign of God's light in every heart that believes. It is not far away; it is here, living inside you. The manger was the doorway, and your heart has become the throne. This Kingdom does not rise or fall with time, for it was founded on Christ Himself. The same light that filled the heavens now fills His people. Wherever peace reigns, wherever love leads, the Kingdom shines. You are not waiting to enter it—you are already living in its glow.

The Shining Kingdom cannot be measured in gold or land. It is seen in mercy, heard in kindness, and felt in grace. Every time you forgive, Heaven rules. Every time you love, Heaven expands. You carry the Kingdom's light in your thoughts, your words, and your actions. The same glory that surrounded the angels now surrounds you. You are a citizen of Heaven, walking the earth with the light of eternity in your eyes. The world may not see crowns or castles, but Heaven sees the King's reflection in you.

Jesus said, "The Kingdom of God is within you." That truth was born in the stable and confirmed at the cross. The Shining Kingdom is not built outside—it grows from within. It is the peace that never breaks, the joy that never ends, and the life that never fades. You do not wait for Heaven to arrive; Heaven already reigns in your spirit. Wherever you walk in love, the Kingdom moves. Wherever you speak truth, its light breaks through the shadows. You are part of its everlasting glow.

The Shining Kingdom is a family of light. Its people are joined by faith, not by walls or distance. Every believer across the world shines with the same presence. Together, they form the body of Christ—a living Kingdom of glory spreading through every generation. You are part of that family. The King lives in you, and His light joins with the light of others, making the world glow brighter each day. His Kingdom knows no end because His love has no limit.

Even when darkness tries to rise, the Kingdom shines stronger. Its foundation cannot be shaken. Its peace cannot be stolen. The Shining Kingdom stands on the power of God's Word, and that Word lives in you. Every act of faith declares that Christ reigns. Every word of truth reveals His crown. You do not represent a Kingdom to come—you reveal the one that already is. The light in you is its banner, and the peace in you is its anthem.

Now rest, child of the King. The Shining Kingdom is your home, and its light covers you completely. The same glory that filled Bethlehem's night fills your heart tonight. Sleep knowing that you belong to a Kingdom without end, ruled by love, and radiant with His presence.

Day 27: The Forever Morning

When Jesus was born, the light of Heaven broke the horizon, and the world would never see night the same way again. That morning never ended—it became The Forever Morning. Every sunrise since that day has carried the promise that light has won. The darkness may try to return, but it cannot overcome the dawn that Christ began. The Forever Morning is not only for Bethlehem; it is for every heart that believes. You live in that endless sunrise, where hope never fades, joy never ends, and love never sleeps. The same glory that filled the first morning fills your heart each day you awaken in His light.

The Forever Morning is God's way of saying, "I am with you always." It reminds you that His mercy never runs out and His peace never closes its eyes. The dawn that began in a manger still spreads across the earth through every believer. Each act of kindness adds to its brightness. Each prayer, each song, each moment of faith lifts the light higher. You are part of that sunrise—its warmth lives in your words, and its glow shines through your life. You do not wait for the light to return; you are already standing in it.

Even when clouds fill the sky, the morning still reigns. The sun does not disappear when you cannot see it, and neither does His presence. The Forever Morning is stronger than any shadow. You may face challenges, but they cannot dim His joy. His light is constant, His love unbreakable. Every day you wake is another reminder that resurrection power lives in you. The morning that rose over the empty tomb is the same light that fills your spirit now. You live in the dawn that never ends.

The world may mark time by days and nights, but Heaven knows only morning. In Christ, every moment is lit by His glory. The Forever Morning means that the Son never sets. His light watches over you when you sleep and greets you when you rise. You are never in the dark, because the Light of the world has made His home in you. Every breath you take carries His brightness, and every heartbeat echoes His victory. The morning of His mercy will shine forever.

The angels rejoiced that first dawn, but Heaven still rejoices now. Every life touched by His light becomes another ray of the same eternal morning. You are not a shadowed soul—you are part of the sunrise. You are the evidence that darkness is defeated, that life has triumphed, and that love reigns forever. The Forever Morning is your inheritance, your reality, your song.

Now rest, child of light, under the glow of His endless day. The Forever Morning shines over you even in the night. Its warmth fills your dreams, its peace guards your heart. The same light that began in Bethlehem still rises in you. Sleep knowing that the dawn will never fade, for you live in the light of The Forever Morning.

Day 28: The Star Still Shines

The night sky over Bethlehem once glowed with a single Star that marked the arrival of the Savior. That light has never gone out. The Star Still Shines because Christ still lives. Though ages have passed and kingdoms have fallen, His glory remains bright and unchanging. What began as a light over a stable has become a light in every heart that believes. The same brightness that led wise men to the manger now leads His people in truth. The Star Still Shines, not in the heavens above alone, but in the hearts below—where His love burns without end.

The world may change, but His light does not. Storms may pass, seasons may turn, but the flame of His presence is eternal. The Star still shines over those who trust in Him, guiding, healing, restoring. It reminds the world that God has not withdrawn His promise. Every sunrise, every act of love, every word of grace is proof that the same light that filled the stable still fills the earth. Christ in you is the star that never fades, the glory that no darkness can cover. You are the living reflection of His eternal dawn.

The Star still shines because His work is finished, and His love is complete. When He came, He brought Heaven to earth. When He rose, He made that light unbreakable. You are part of that victory. His presence in you is the light of the world continuing to glow through generations. Every time you forgive, every time you speak peace, the Star shines again. You do not carry a flicker—you carry the brilliance of His truth, steady and strong. The light is not waiting to return; it has already conquered the night.

Even when life feels dim, the Star still shines. Its glow is not dependent on your strength but on His faithfulness. The same Spirit that hovered over Bethlehem now hovers over you, whispering peace and filling you with warmth. No darkness can overcome this light, for it is the very presence of God Himself. Wherever you go, the world sees the reflection of His glory in your life. You are His living constellation—proof that Emmanuel has come and will never leave.

Heaven rejoices every time His light shines through you. The angels who sang that first night still celebrate each time a heart remembers His love. You were born into a world already lit by His victory. You are part of the same story, carrying the same flame. The Star that shone once above now shines within you—unending, unwavering, unstoppable.

Now rest, little one, in the glow that never fades. The Star Still Shines above you, around you, and within you. Its light guards your dreams and fills your heart with peace. Christ has come, Christ remains, and Christ reigns. The Star Still Shines—and because He lives in you, so do you shine forever.

List of Titles Included in This Collection

Children's Bedtime Series

1. *The Star That Shines in You, ISBN: 9781970550115, Trim: 5x8, Catalog: A990*

2. *The Shepherd's Whisper, ISBN: 9781970550016, Trim: 5x8, Catalog: A991*

3. *The Gift No One Could Wrap, ISBN: 9781970550023, Trim: 5x8, Catalog: A992*

Parable Series

4. *The Carpenter's Lantern, ISBN: 9781970550030, Trim: 4x6, Catalog: A993*

5. *The Innkeeper's Secret Room, ISBN: 9781970550047, Trim: 4x6, Catalog: A994*

6. *The Donkey That Knew the King, ISBN: 9781970550054, Trim: 4x6, Catalog: A995*

Family Series

7. *You Carry Heaven's Joy, ISBN: 9781970550061, Trim: 5x8, Catalog: A996*

8. *You Shine Brighter Than the Star, ISBN: 9781970550078, Trim: 5x8, Catalog: A997*

9. *You Speak Like Angels Sang, ISBN: 9781970550085, Trim: 5x8, Catalog: A998*

10. *You Bring Peace on Earth, ISBN: 9781970550092, Trim: 5x8, Catalog: A999*

www.ingramcontent.com/pod-product-compliance
Lightning Source LLC
Chambersburg PA
CBHW061715120626
46550CB00003B/1230